Our First Orange President

By Sean Seville

Table of Contents

Dedications:

I dedicate this book to my mother, Diane Spivey. The only person that has acknowledged my creativity and ability to write. She continues to do so in a positive manner.

Thank you

Acknowledgements:

The swamp of Washington D.C.
The cartoon characters that continue to run the country.

When Ned Met Carrie Mann

A divine fairy tale of sorts. A chance meeting that led to an unexpected romance. Finding that special someone. Falling in love, never separating from your essential life partner. This is the stuff that dreams are made of...unfortunately this is not that type of story. Not by a long shot.

For you see, this is a tale of evil, abhorrent individuals, the avariciously inclined, and poor judgment. This involves two people that should never have met in the first place. Ned Dump was the son of wealthy German immigrants. Later in life after the great World War, it was revealed that they were actually Nazi sympathizers. Thank goodness that they're now deceased.

Like his father before him, Ned was a bigot. He invested in real estate, refusing to rent property to Blacks and Puerto Ricans. After all, lawsuits will come and go, but racism is forever. It can be said, indubitably, that Ned was a despicable, conniving man that had a propensity for gambling, booze, and reasonably priced hookers. Dump's sexual appetite was satiated with the company of subpar escorts with very little talent. Despite being nowhere near top of the line they did get the job done.

Alcohol was sufficient in numbing Ned's senses. Dump often felt that bargain basement streetwalkers were beneath him, but sometimes a man has to settle and take a break from working hard as a degenerate. One dark and dreary evening, Ned decided to go for a walk. It was for an urgent matter, indeed. Dump was in need of finding his dealer. Perish the thought of him going one more night without any opium to smoke.

Suddenly it began to drizzle. In fear of his attire becoming far too damp, Ned picked up his pace and made haste. He hurried across the street, and as soon as Dump stepped onto the sidewalk, a young woman bumped into him. Both of these individuals stared at one another.

"I beg your pardon," the young lady said. "My name is Carrie Mann. I'm new to this country. Just trying to get home and out of the rain."

As a young immigrant from Scotland, America can be seen as an enormous, prosperous land that one would yearn to explore. Ned promptly introduced himself and offered Carrie Mann the opportunity to accompany him to meet his dealer. Foolishly, the young woman accepted Dump's less than benevolent offer. Together the two scurried away like possums, to acquire the narcotics.

A few years later they got married. Before long they had offspring. Five children in total. None were as detestable as child number four. It was a dreadful day in June when this hellspawn was given birth. It was prophesied to bring about the end of the world.

Ned Dump was a horrible human being. Not fit to be a role model by any means. The little one did not require any encouragement for wrong doing. It all came naturally. Carrie Mann was ashamed of what she had done, to provide a helping hand in forging imminent Armageddon.

This woman could not be devoid of blame. She had ample opportunity to get an abortion. This "mother of mayhem" could've had every ounce of demonic matter that she carried within her womb, vacuumed and cleared of all evil presence. This action would have prevented a future in which an insufferable plague in the form of one human being rises to power, and sends mankind spiraling into utter destruction, and an inferno of burning brimstone and rubble. For the part that Carrie Mann the witch played, she deserved to be burned alive at the stake.

Hell on Earth had cometh. A horrible, little, orange ogre named Ronald T. Dump was born. God have mercy...

The Führer

He was most
pleased to get
cookies and ice cream
after the conclusion of
his first presidential
debate.

The RON

So much can be said regarding Ronald Take a Dump. Ned would pay some of the other parents, so that their children would play with his son. Starting at a young age, Ronald wasn't very likable and a far cry from affable. Soon enough, children that played with young Dump began to demand raises in their salaries. Ned already paid the parents well, but the children did not always see the fruit of their labor.

They were suffering and demanded a larger cut of the pie. Tension began to build as the children were forced to spend more time with Ronald. He would steal toys from everyone and declare them as his property. His storytelling abilities were made apparent at age ten, when Ronald would explain to the others that Indians landed on Plymouth Rock, and his savior Andrew Jackson slaughtered them all just in time for Thanksgiving dinner. Even back then, Ronald would construct his world of make believe, and convert it into his own form of reality.

Unfortunately, he progressively became worse with age. His older siblings didn't want anything to do with him. They could smell the bullshit emanating from Ronald every time he entered the room. So many despicable deeds were committed by "The Ronald" throughout his adulthood, such as having people work on extensive and exhausting building projects and then never paying them for their labor. Opening a college where students paid extremely high tuition fees, and instead of eventually earning degrees, they only received a lesson in the "school of hard knocks."

Later Ronald wrote a book entitled: Art Of The Rip Off. This of course was an aptly named piece of literature. Dump's refusal to rent or sell property to minorities was certainly something that daddy could be proud of. Let it be known that this list could go on and on. A record of "accolades" in the warped mind of one Ronald T. Dump.

A Competent President

After eight years of the country coping with a foolish imbecile in the oval office, the time had come to elect a new president. Long fierce campaign battles were waged. One man of determination emerged victorious and his name was Harmack Labamba. As a positive role model to the youth, he could make them believe that even in times of turmoil change is possible. To say that his popularity had skyrocketed was a slight understatement.

It was during the third year of his tenure as president, Harmack headlined the white house correspondent's association dinner. Among others, an invitation by a local newspaper press was given out to no other than Ronald Take a Dump. Mr. Dump did not hesitate to attend the dinner. That evening, Harmack stood before the podium on stage, and commenced roasting Ronald for approximately five minutes.

Harmack's jokes ranged from Dump's repugnant reality show to his asinine conspiracy theories. Afterwards, a famous comedian decided to join in on the fun, and mock Ronald's lustrous mane of hair. (ha, ha, tee, hee) Dump despised Labamba. He was everything that Dump wasn't. This night would go on to serve as a super villain's origin story.

For it was at this very moment that Ronald T. Dump would forge plans to exact his revenge. A petty man vowed to run for the presidency of the United States Of America, and that he did. Approximately eighteen months before the end of Labamba's second term, Dump announced his candidacy for the highest office in the land. Throughout the years, Lambamba was praised by many and beloved by all.

Near the end of his final year as commander in chief, the dawn of a new election was upon us.

Harmack's party nominee for president of the United States lacked in popularity. Some would describe her as stone cold. She had all of the charisma of a T 1000. Never the less this nominee would go on to challenge Ronald Dump in a race to become the next potus.

Fortunately for Ronald, he had friends in very high places. One in particular just happened to be the leader of a powerful foreign government. His name is Cassimir Lieutin. This communist dictator does whatever he can to ensure his reelection is imminent and democracy will never prevail. Lieutin was more than aware that having a man like Ronald Dump as the American President can only work to his advantage.

A puppet with strings can easily be pulled. The notion of America becoming a country that lacks the power and desire of preventing the spread of Cassimir's ideology and agenda had mass appeal to the foreign dictator. Lieutin assisted Dump by interfering in the election. With his help, Dump emerged victorious. Ronald would now lay claim as the most powerful man in the world.

1600 Pennsylvania Avenue
Presidential Bathroom
   Heavy Weight Title Bout... On the toilet
The President is Currently Losing.....

Dump's Revenge

Back when he was on the campaign trail, Dump did his best to appeal to every bigoted, homophobic, hate mongrel currently living. He was endorsed by ex (and current) KKK members and leaders of Nazi regimes. Dump pledged to keep illegal immigrants from entering the country. He oftentimes ejaculated to the mere thought of building a big beautiful wall to get the job done.

After the election it became evident that the fuehrer had risen. Steadily he gained power throughout his tenure in office. As racial tension continued to gain traction, Ronald made sure that his other priorities were not neglected. With the help of his political party controlled congress, Dump passed a 1.3 trillion dollar tax cut that only the wealthiest Americans could benefit from. Ronald Dump was relentless in his crusade.

The fuehrer did everything in his power to erase virtually every achievement that Harack Labamba ever made as president. Dump diligently worked so not a single trace of Labamba's legacy was left. Not even his wife's "Kids Eat Healthy Lunches At School" initiative.

Duh, Duh, Duh, Duh...

Dump's Revenge The Song

♪*Duh, Duh, Duh, Duh,* ♪

♪*What an awful orange man with a peculiar hairstyle* ♪

♪ *Nothing of substance to say/* ♪

♪*With a mouth running mile after mile* ♪

♪*Does everything he can to make* ♪

♪*America somber and grim* ♪

♪*His own niece wrote a book on how much* ♪

♪ *she despises him* ♪

♪*It was completely warranted of course/Ronald* ♪

♪*has no remorse* ♪

♪*His claim that a certain pornstar has* ♪

♪*the face of a horse* ♪

♪*If that is the case/ For goodness sake* ♪

♪*Why did you spend an exorbitant* ♪

♪*amount of money just to pound her cake?* ♪

♪ *Duh, Duh, Duh, Duh, Duh, Duh,* ♪

♪Duh da, Duh da, Duh da, Duh da,♪

♪Da, Da, Da♪

♪Ronald's fat and he's stupid/ Struck♪

♪by an arrow from Cupid/ He's shootin'♪

♪Fell in love with a man named Vladimir/♪

♪Last name is...♪

♪Indulges in fantasies/ Wizards, warlocks, and mages♪

♪Separates families at the borders/Places♪

♪children in cages♪

♪His tale is a tale to tell for the ages♪

♪A manifestation of evil in various stages♪

♪His moronic two oldest sons are a couple of chumps♪

♪ALL SIEG HEIL, RONALD T. DUMP!!!♪

♪Duh, Duh, Duh Duh, Duh Duh,♪

♪Da, Da, Da,♪

♪Duh Duh, Duh Duh, Duh Duh,♪

♪Da, Da, Da,♪

♪When it comes to assisting the common man,♪

♪Dump is more than hesitant♪

♪Only provides tax cuts for the top one percent♪

♪A devastating hurricane hit Puerto Rico/♪

♪Ronald was flown in♪

♪He tossed rolls of paper towels to people♪

♪as if he were feeding dolphins♪

♪Cats or dogs/any animals at the zoo♪

♪Dump felt like he stepped in something and♪

♪it was stuck to the bottom of his shoe♪

♪Doesn't want to help people of color/♪

♪This he has sworn♪

♪This is hypocritical of course because♪

♪he is orange!♪

♪Duh Duh, Duh Duh, Duh Duh,♪

♪Da, Da, Da,♪

♪Duh Duh, Duh Duh, Duh Duh,♪

♪Da, Da, Da....♪

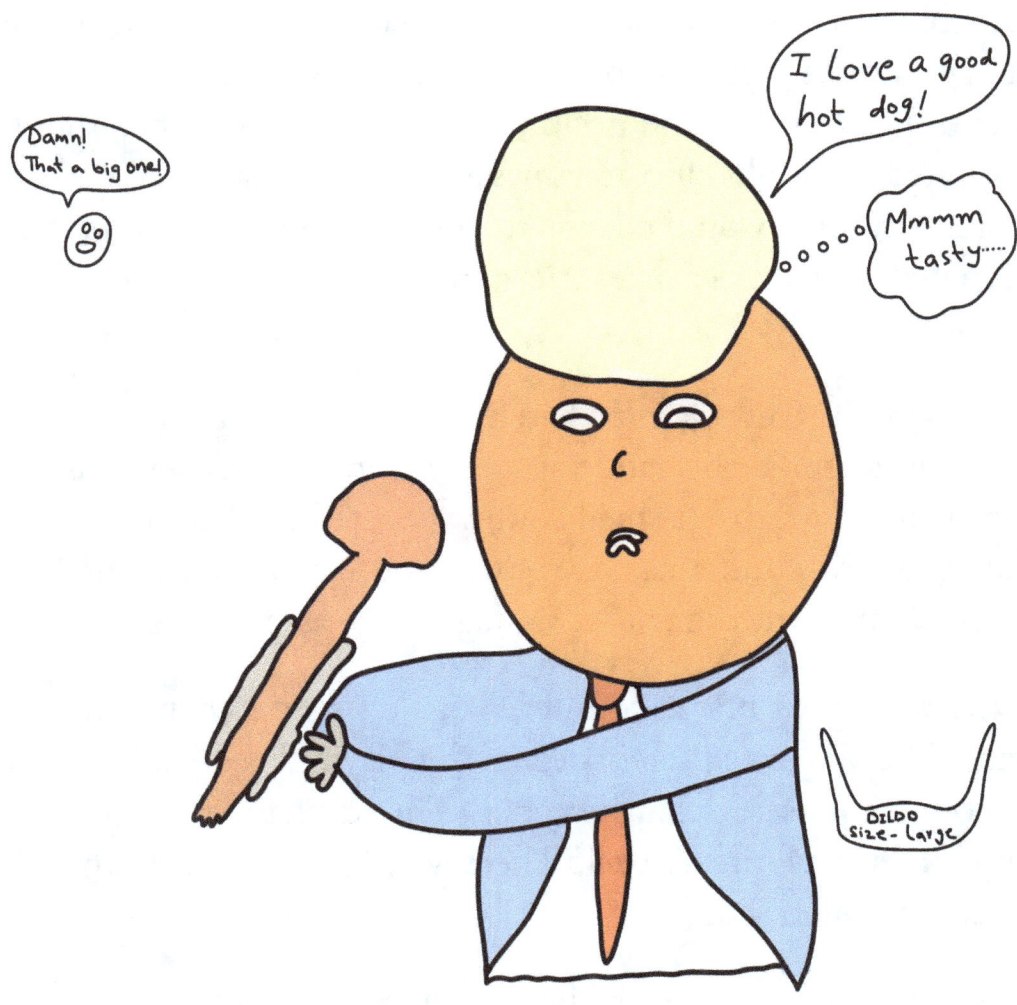

Love Is Where You Find It

On the subject of love, how can such a thing exist for a monster that is incapable of comprehending the mere concept? After a couple of failed marriages that produced a total of four bastard offspring, Ronald became disheartened in the notion of love. One night he attended a party located in a night club at Times Square. Fate had stretched out its unkind hand, for it would change the life of one woman in particular. This is where Ronald met an exotic, gorgeous underwear model named, Fradonnia.

At her core she truly wasn't a bad human being, but sometimes poor judgment leads to Earth shattering consequences. Fradonnia is an immigrant from Slovenia. A small country located in Central Europe. It is known for its mountains, ski resorts, and lakes. When the climate becomes warmer, one can take advantage of the astonishing hot springs.

A week after their first encounter, Ronald began to court this young woman. The ogre often serenaded her by playing records. Works from the famous composer Richard Wagner. This just happened to be one of Adolph Hitler's favorites as well. There were late nights with the couple stretched out on the couch.

Consideration would get the best of Dump. He allowed Fradonnia to pick and remove all of the lint and grit from his exposed belly button. What a lucky gal, indeed. Five years passed since their initial meeting. The couple were married in Palm Beach. Fradonnia thought she was starting a new life with an intelligent, real estate mogul.

I suppose that when you have your head held high and your eyes closed, one doesn't expect to be decapitated by the spinning rotor blades of a standing helicopter. It just sort of happens. Before long, Fradonnia gave birth to yet another "Spawn of Satan." Fradonnia was far from happy. In due time her life had taken a turn for the worse.

It was Never love at First Sight!
Man's Got to eat! Apparently Never exercise

The Great Russian Hope

During the first year of his term, President Dump met Cassimir Lieutin. Their encounter had been scheduled as a part of the G20 summit in Hamburg. It was shrouded in secrecy, and lasted for over two hours. The only other people present were there language translators, and both American and Russian foreign ministers. Such a magical rendezvous if ever there was one.

Later that evening, Dump approached Lieutin and the two of them spoke privately and animatedly for almost an hour. The truth of the matter is, Cassimir is capable of speaking some English, but he preferred for this not to become public knowledge. The only other person present was Lieutin's translator. Immediately sparks flew. Their relationship had begun, and it didn't take long for it to intensify. Frequent night visitations were made between the two.

Sometimes Dump would travel to the Kremlin under the guise of addressing foreign policies. On other occasions, Dump would help Lieutin sneak into the White House for a "sleep over." Fradonnia was never the wiser, or was she? One night Cassimir laid in bed waiting for his queen. Dump emerged from the bathroom wearing a freshly pressed Gestapo uniform. He marched toward the bed, declaring several SIEG HEILS before laying down.

Dump ordered Lieutin to lick his boots but he refused. Lieutin felt insulted and got out of bed. Ronald quickly chased after him. Lieutin spoke in Russian. "I grow weary of these games," he said.

Cassimir pulled down Ronald's leather chaps and bent him over the nearby sofa. Subsequently the men engaged in rough butt sex for the entirety of twelve whole minutes. Dump craved more but Cassimir was getting old.

However, the Soviet Ruler was considerate enough to ejaculate in Dump's Dumper this time and not his face. After all, the Cold War was over.

This was something that literally made Ronald feel warm inside. The President was smitten. Nothing says, "I love you" like the kind of sodomy that leaves you bleeding for more. Those that became aware of the illicit affair were compelled to keep their mouths shut. There were stormy nights when Dump was alone and strongly felt Cassimir's absence.

All he can do is lay on the floor and play with his choo choo trains. It wasn't difficult for the President to cheer himself up. He would take initiative, get on Twitter to bully and mock young teenage activists. He didn't have anything better to do...except run the country. These antics would tire Ronald so.

He fell significantly deep into slumber. Dreams now festered in his mind. Within the confines of his subconscious, there was a "dirty dance" sequence. At the end he leaped into the big strong hands and muscular build of his betrothed. Dump was held up high in a swan position. Similar to a particular movie.

A moment later, Dump became seventeen years of age, again. His parents were berating him. The Russian President stepped in and confronted the father. "Nobody puts Ronald in the corner," Cassimir said (In Russian of course). The next morning Dump had awakened with a smile on his face, as he hugged his pillow tightly.

It was one for the ages. A long distance relationship that had all the love and flair of a backed up sewer. Regardless, there is never a day that goes by when Dump doesn't yearn for the most uncharismatic Russian Leader.

Fradonnia's Wishes

It was a breezy night with a slight chill, during which a man proceeded to lay his woman down on top of an enormous bed covered with rose pedals. Such a soft, plush mattress. The silk sheets seemed to cling to the woman's legs that glistened in the moonlight. Then came forth an unyielding embrace as passionate kisses followed. What a whirlwind of delight and sensual conquest.

The lust and desire felt by this woman only increased by each passing moment. Sweat began to trickle down her lover's brow as their conclave of intimacy carried on. The woman in all of her years had never engaged in sheer ecstasy of this magnitude. A series of random then eventually well coordinated encounters with this gentleman that she hardly knew, yet had known of him fairly well, finally culminated in love making of immense proportions. But is it true?

She wondered to herself. Is it actually love she desired or merely lust in disguise, wrapped up with a tightly bound ribbon presented to her by the gods themselves? Perhaps it didn't matter in the least. She finally had what she craved more than anything. Something that would not be taken for granted.

Her "knight in shining armor" is here to stay. At the end that's all that matters. It all seemed surreal. The woman could not begin to fathom how such fortuitous circumstances have come to be. She always wanted Labamba and finally...

Suddenly Fradonnia awoke from her slumber. The orange ogre refused to remain dormant in his chamber located in the lower part of

Dump Towers. Quickly walking with a gait, but without hesitation, he snatched up his wife as if she were a mere piece of fruit. Was the peril even real? This poor woman.

Did her life truly hang in the balance? Fradonnia was certainly unable to escape the clutches of this orange fiend. Heavy steps were taken as the ogre carried the woman over his shoulder He then ascended the winding, spiral staircase. Eventually this monstrous creature reached the top of Dump Towers, the 58th floor. He opened the door of the lavish and luxurious penthouse.

With haste, Fradonnia was pushed inside. After which, the door slammed shut and locked from the outside. Footsteps from the ogre soon receded back down the stairs. As former underwear model turned princess held in captivity, Fradonnia was hardly content with her current predicament. She stepped out onto the patio, and then leaned slightly over the balcony railing. Despite feeling distraught she did not give up hope.

Once she stretched her left arm forward, a little blue jay landed on the open palm of her hand. The princess felt compelled to sing...

Fradonnia's Wishes The Song

♪I'm a timid little flower, trapped in an ivory tower♪

♪Married to a horrid ogre/ Causes me to cringe and cower♪

♪Behind these very walls I fidget/ Every hour, every minute♪

♪Ronald's persistent/ He likes to touch me/♪

♪I wish he would quit it♪

♪Cannot bear to lay eyes on his leathery face♪

♪and now I'm on pace♪

♪When push comes to shove♪

♪I will spray him with mace♪

♪An insipid troll/ In defense,♪

♪I'll stomp on his toes♪

♪Pull Ronald's hanging scrotum all the♪

♪way up to his nose♪

♪La, La, Hee, Hee,La, Lee, Lo, Lay♪

♪Hi, Ha, Ho, Ha,Maybe Someday♪

♪Tick Tock The Clock Is Running♪

♪Lo, La, Ho, Ho,By The Way♪

♪For where art thou?/ The man I truly desire♪

♪Altruistic, has integrity/ He sets my heart on fire♪

♪I'm trying not to swoon/ Somebody please help!♪

♪My husband won't stop making an ass of himself♪

♪Labamba cares for his constituents♪

♪unlike someone else that I know♪

♪I have to change the ogre's diapers♪

♪before his rallies/ It truly is a shit show♪

♪I've been patiently waiting for my prince/♪

♪When is he coming?/ I wanna/♪

♪Flee far away from this place with♪

♪former President Labamba♪

♪La, La, Hee, Hee,La, Lee, Lo, Lay,♪

♪Ho, Ho, Ha, Ho, Maybe Someday♪

♪Tick Tock The Clock Is Running♪

♪La, Lo, Ho, Ho,By The Way♪

♪No one challenges Ronald when♪

♪she goes to the playground ♪

♪He brings armed National Guards to ♪

♪show who's in charge♪

♪The children hate him and face♪

♪him when they start throwing rocks♪

♪Dump orders the secret service,♪

♪shoot to kill/So he can play alone in the sandbox♪

♪I don't want to catch a cold or other♪

♪things from when he coughs or sneezes♪

♪Ronald sleeps with a great many♪

♪whores with venereal diseases♪

♪He's repulsive and crude/ Crass and quite rude♪

♪I'm at a loss/ I don't know what to do♪

♪La, La, Hee, Hee,La, Lee, Lo, Lay,♪

♪Ha Ha, Ho, Ha, Maybe Someday♪

♪Tick Tock The Clock Is Running♪

♪La, La, Ho, Ho,By The Way...♪

Princess Fradonnia fell silent. A tear fell from her eye as she gazed at the passing clouds. Maybe someday indeed, the man that she adores will come and whisk her away from this wretched place. Sometimes fairytales do come true. Although, Fradonnia's knight is already married, and has two kids. Therefore, this dream turning into reality is a little unlikely...

January
6th

January 6, 20xx

A Day Of Infamy

On January 6, 20XX Dump supporters arrived in droves at the U.S. State Capitol. Their goal was to keep Dump in power by the prevention of electoral votes being counted, which would solidify President Elect Bo Triden's victory in the latest election. Many of these supporters could be heard shouting and screaming. Ultimately, they broke into the U.S. Capitol Building and ran amok.

They began to laugh and sing as they called for the head of Vice President Ike Mince. The hunt was on. The insurrectionists were adamant about finding the V.P. and executing him for committing "An act of treason."

Dump Supporters Sing

♪We'll provide a public hanging for the VP♪

♪And that's just what he'll do♪

♪Mince will dance at the end of a rope♪

♪Giving us a jig or two♪

♪Eyes will bulge far from his head/♪

♪Like in the cartoons♪

♪Don't breathe too hard and give♪

♪away your hiding spot because♪

♪that will spell your doom...♪

Meanwhile, Mince did his best to remain hidden inside the closet at the State Capitol Building, as Dump supporters searched frantically for the embroiled Vice President. He cowered and quivered as tears began to freefall from his eyes.

As all of this transpired, Dump masturbated to the sight of 2500 insurrectionists storming the U.S. Capitol. Shouts of condemnation toward a government that would dare remove Dump from power. This was music to Ronald's ears. He didn't miss a moment. Dump's eyes remained glued to the television, and a different type of adhesive to his hand.

Jan 6, 20xx

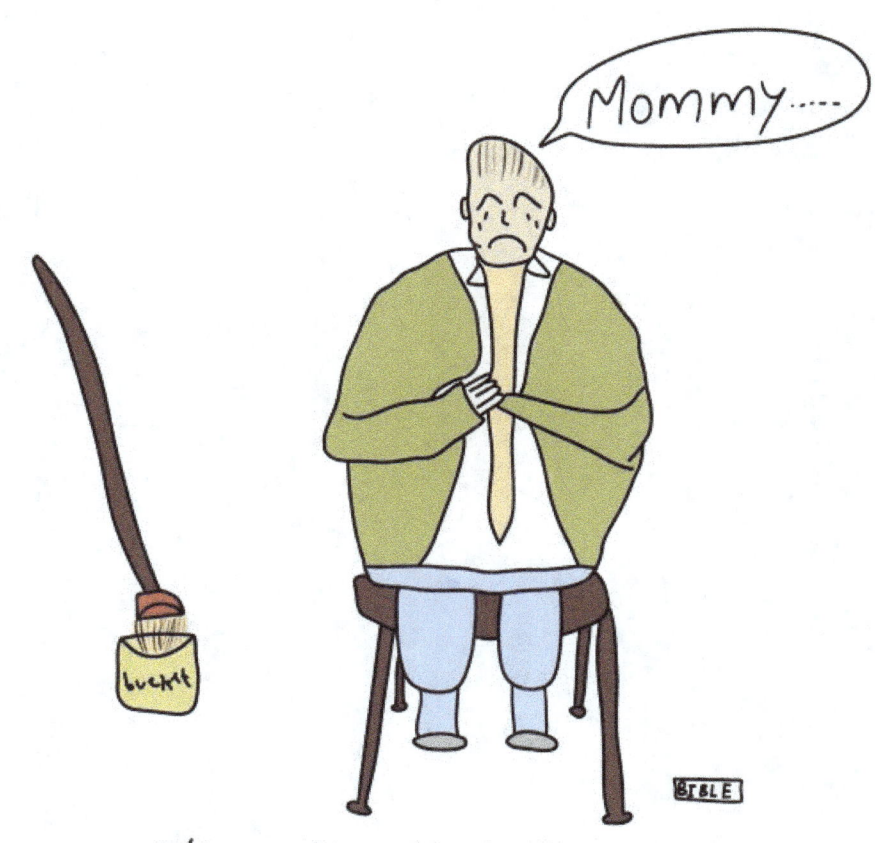

Vice President IKE Mince

EPILOGUE

On January 20, 20XX Ronald T. Dump left the White House along with his hostage...I mean wife, Fradonnia. His term might be over, but the world hasn't heard the last of Dump...

Our First Orange President

About The Author:

Sean Seville is an author/entertainer from Chicago, Illinois